THE OFFICIAL WEST BROMWICH ALBION ANNUAL 2017

A Grange Publication

Written by Dave Bowler
Designed by B. Scott-Peterson

©2016. Published by Grange Communications Ltd., Edinburgh, under licence from West Bromwich Albion Football Club. Printed in the EU.

Every effort has been made to ensure the accuracy of information within this publication but the publishers cannot be held responsible for any errors or omissions. Views expressed are those of the author and do not necessarily represent those of the publishers or the football club.

All rights reserved.

Photographs © West Bromwich Albion Football Club and Action Images.

ISBN 978-1-911287-16-2

CONTENTS

- 6   Head Coach
- 7   Crossword
- 8   Season Review
- 18 2015/2016 Match Stats
- 20 All Change!
- 22 Download Albion!
- 23 Word Search
- 24 Dinner Party… With Craig Dawson
- 25 Nacer to Fly Albion to the Moon!
- 26 This Year's Model!
- 28 Summertime, and the Living is Easy
- 32 Player of the Season - Darren Fletcher
- 34 The Big Albion Quiz: The Premier League Years
- 35 Allan's Key to Albion Hopes
- 36 Here, There & Everywhere!
- 38 Our Ball, But Which One?
- 39 My First: Chris Brunt
- 40 My Favourite Game
- 42 Looking to Make his Mark
- 43 He's One of Our Own
- 45 Hal's on Target at the Hawthorns
- 46 Albion at the Euros
- 48 Baggies Bag Toffee
- 49 It's You Rondon-Don, It's You Rondon!
- 51 The Key Question!
- 52 Player Profiles
- 60 Goal of the Season
- 61 Quiz and Puzzle Answers

HEAD COACH

AFTER A SPELL WHERE ALBION WERE CHANGING HEAD COACH PRETTY FREQUENTLY, Tony Pulis has brought some stability to The Hawthorns.

Having steered Albion away from relegation troubles and to safety after taking over in January 2015, it was a much calmer season for the Baggies in 2015/16 as we stayed well out of trouble right the way to the end of the season.

Tony has been a manager for nearly 25 years now and early in the 2016/17 season, he is set to register the 1,000th game in his career, a milestone that very few managers ever reach.

Wearing his trademark baseball cap, Pulis is instantly recognisable on the touchline and in the dugout, where his experience has helped the Baggies re-establish ourselves as a proper Premier League team to be reckoned with!

CROSSWORD

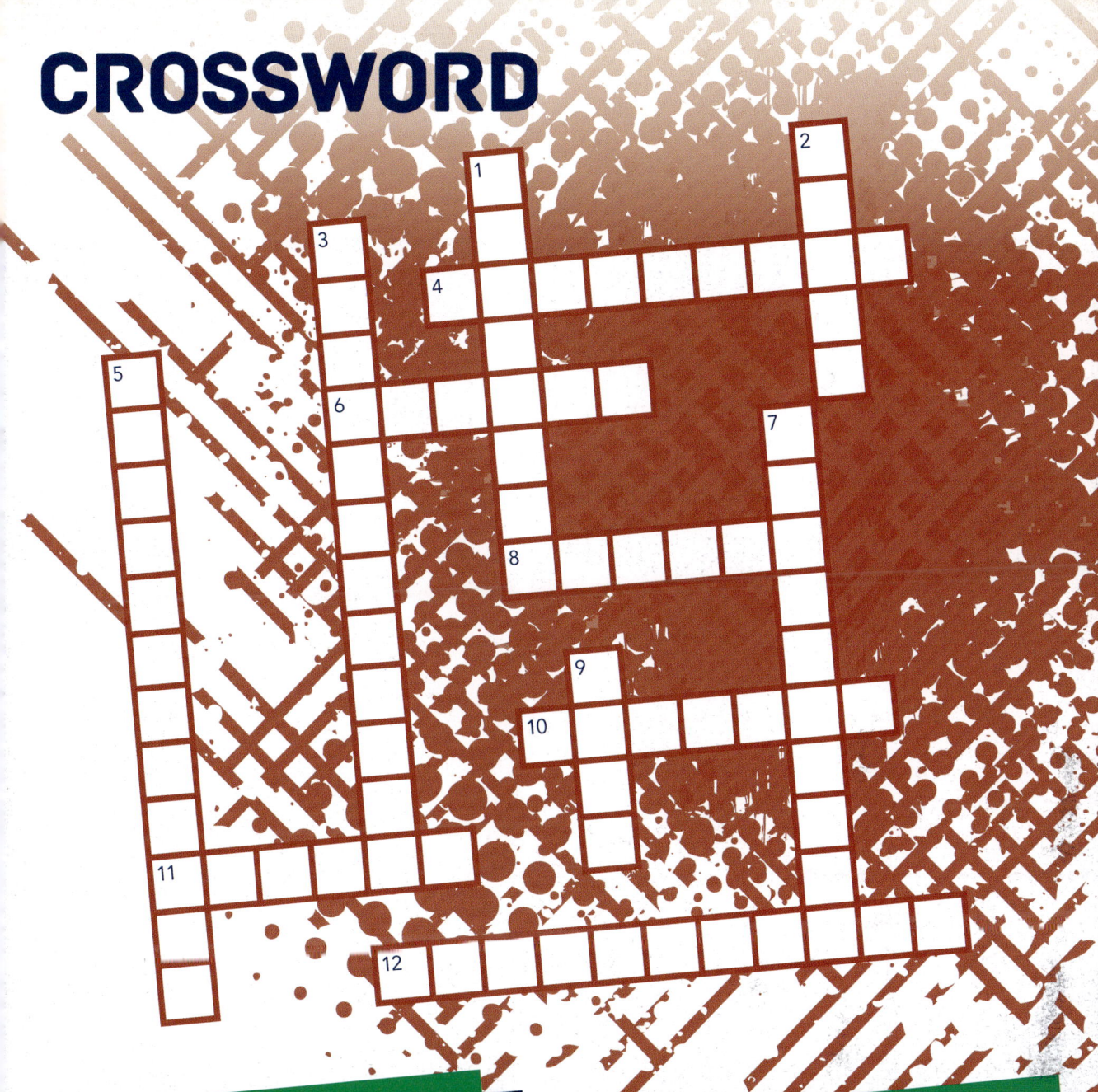

ACROSS

4. IT'S OPPOSITE THE BRUMMIE!
6. WEST BROMWICH…WHAT?
8. THE SKIPPER'S FIRST NAME
10. COME ON YOU…WHO?
11. SUPER SALOMON
12. HE'S BEEN OUR NUMBER 25 FOR A FEW YEARS NOW

DOWN

1. ACADEMY MIDFIELDER WHO MADE HIS DEBUT AGAINST LIVERPOOL
2. CLAUDIO'S MAGIC YOU KNOW
3. ALBION'S YOUNG PLAYER OF THE SEASON
5. YOUNG WELSH STRIKER WHO MADE HIS DEBUT AGAINST LIVERPOOL
7. NORTHERN IRISH DEFENDER WE BOUGHT FROM MANCHESTER UNITED
9. THE BEST SHADE OF BLUE!

Answers on p.61

SEASON REVIEW

AUGUST

A long summer without any football finally ended when, on a Monday night, Manchester City started the season with a visit to The Hawthorns. The game ended in a 3-0 defeat but we responded well to that by going to newly promoted Watford and digging out a 0-0 draw in a carnival atmosphere at Vicarage Road.

The games didn't get any easier at The Hawthorns as we welcomed reigning champions Chelsea for game three. It was a real cracker too. James Morrison missed a penalty but scored two goals anyway, John Terry was sent off, but Chelsea held on and won a terrific game 3-2.

The Capital One Cup was up next and although new signing Rickie Lambert had two blockbusting attempts at goal from long distance, our tie with Port Vale went all the way to penalties after a 0-0 draw, James Chester finally winning the shootout for us.

Then it was off to Stoke City for one of the more bizarre afternoons of the season as the Potters had two men sent off and Albion's record signing, Salomon Rondon, headed in a Lambert cross to register his first goal for the club and win the game.

SEPTEMBER

After the season's first international break, we returned with a 0-0 draw against Southampton and then we had the first really big day out of the year when we went to Villa Park and avenged the previous season's defeat, Saido Berahino scoring the only goal of a game that we might have won by five or six!

It was a long, long trip in midweek to Norwich City to lose in the Capital One Cup but things looked better a few days later when we were 2-0 up at home to Everton under the floodlights. But those lights obviously woke up Everton's Romelu Lukaku – remember him? – and by the end of the game, Everton won 3-2.

OCTOBER

Last season, one of our best wins was away at Crystal Palace but it was very different this time around as we struggled and were well beaten 2-0. Once again, we were up for the challenge of doing better next time and came away with a 1-0 win over Sunderland, with Sam Allardyce taking his first game as their manager. Another Berahino goal was enough to give us all three points.

It was 1-0 to the Albion again the following Saturday as we made our second visit of the season to Norwich, this time in the league. After peppering the Norwich goal, it was Rondon who popped up to score the all important goal that won the game to take the Baggies shooting up the league table.

Leicester came to The Hawthorns next for a game on Hallowe'en. It was a suitably horrible afternoon for the Albion too as we had a couple of great penalty claims turned down, decisions that turned the game Leicester's way as Jamie Vardy got what turned out to be the winner in a game that finished 3-2 to the Foxes. That win took Leicester to third place in the Premier League, but there was no way they were going to stay that close to the top, was there…

SEASON REVIEW

NOVEMBER

The Theatre of Dreams was our next stop and Albion handled Manchester United well, just a goal behind with a few minutes to go when Saido Berahino missed a great chance to bring things level. From there, United had a quick break in injury time from which Gareth McAuley conceded a penalty and collected a red card, Mata making the game safe for United from the penalty spot.

Tough games are a fact of life in the Premier League and Arsenal were our next opponents after the next international break, this time at The Hawthorns. Following the terrorist attacks in Paris, the teams gathered together before the game to sing the French national anthem. It was Arsenal that started the better, Giroud giving them the lead, but we struck back with a beautiful volleyed goal by Morrison before Arteta turned a James McClean cross into his own net to give Albion all three points.

We were off to London and our final visit to the Boleyn Ground before West Ham's move to the Olympic Stadium. It was a pretty successful way to say farewell, Albion coming from behind to get a second half draw courtesy of a deflected Lambert shot and, like plenty of games during the season, we might have done even better!

SEASON REVIEW

DECEMBER

We carried on playing London teams when title-chasing Tottenham were our first visitors in December. They were on the attack from the start when Dele Alli put them ahead in front of the Birmingham Road End. But fear not, we had James McClean who came racing in at the Smethwick End to bang in a header and get us a draw.

There was another great performance against one of the big clubs when we went to Anfield and came from a goal down to lead Liverpool. despite Jonas Olsson having a goal disallowed, Olsson and Craig Dawson both finding the target as we led 2-1 going into the fifth minute of injury time, before a hugely deflected shot found its way past Boaz Myhill and into the far corner, Jurgen Klopp and his Liverpool players celebrating the draw in front of the Kop as if they'd won the cup.

We had a big crowd at home the week before Christmas for the visit of Bournemouth, but Rondon and McClean got early gifts that they didn't want – a red card each – as Albion slipped to a 2-1 defeat against the Premier League new boys.

There were no presents on Boxing Day either as we were beaten away at Swansea City but Christmas got much better when we enjoyed back-to-back wins at The Hawthorns over the following week. We could have scored half a dozen goals against Newcastle but one was enough in the end, skipper Darren Fletcher's header squirming past Darlow and in.

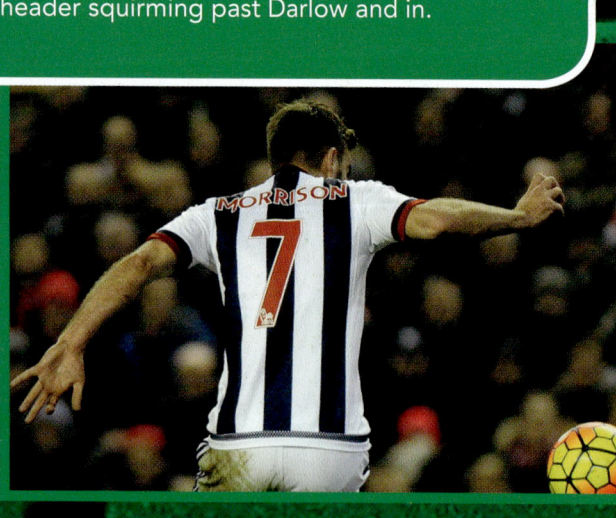

JANUARY

Better yet came when we beat Stoke City at home at the start of 2016 thanks to a goal from Jonny Evans which came with virtually the last kick of the game to make it 2-1 – is there a more exciting way to win a match than with a late, late goal?

Then it was time to start the FA Cup campaign with Ben Foster, returning from injury, in goal. After dominating against Bristol City, we somehow found ourselves losing 2-1 right into the final seconds of injury time before Evans set up Morrison to knock in a vital equaliser.

That was virtually Morrison's last touch of the ball for the season because a few minutes into our next game, at Chelsea, he was taken off injured and didn't play again all season. You'd have thought that would cost us dear at Stamford Bridge but no, substitute Craig Gardner came on, played superbly and scored a brilliant goal. A late McClean strike sealed a 2-2 draw on a night where, once more, we might well have won.

A weary group of players were defeated at Southampton three days later and then we advanced in the FA Cup by beating Bristol City on a freezing night at the newly improved Ashton Gate in our replay. We followed that up with a 0-0 draw at home to Villa that won't live long in anyone's memory and we ended the month by turning another dominant display in the FA Cup against lower division opposition into a 2-2 draw, Peterborough United earning a replay after Berahino scored twice.

FEBRUARY

It was a big night at The Hawthorns when we entertained Swansea City but it took a last gasp equaliser from Rondon to get us the vital point that we deserved against the Welsh side. That set us up for a trip to big-spending Newcastle United as the transfer window closed and despite debuts for our own Alex Pritchard and Sandro, we ended up beaten by the only goal of the game.

A long, long night at Peterborough in the FA Cup followed, Albion finally seeing off the Posh with a 4-3 win on penalties to move into the fifth round. We celebrated by going to Goodison Park on the Saturday and grinding out a really important 1-0 win after Rondon gave us an early lead. Everton had most of the ball but couldn't find our goal and that was three more points in the bag.

It set us up nicely for a trip to Reading in the FA Cup but that turned out to be a grim day for the club, Albion losing 3-1 and Chris Brunt being hit by a coin thrown by a spectator in the Albion end of the ground.

The true Albion fans then rallied round Brunty and collected a lot of money for charity in his name with a bucket collection before the Crystal Palace game. Sadly, that day turned into a nightmare for him too as he was carried off with a knee injury that ruled him out of the rest of the season and the European Championships.

It was a bad note on an otherwise great day as Albion tore Palace to shreds in the first half to lead 3-0 before Palace staged a late fight back to make it 3-2. But those three points put us well clear of the drop zone.

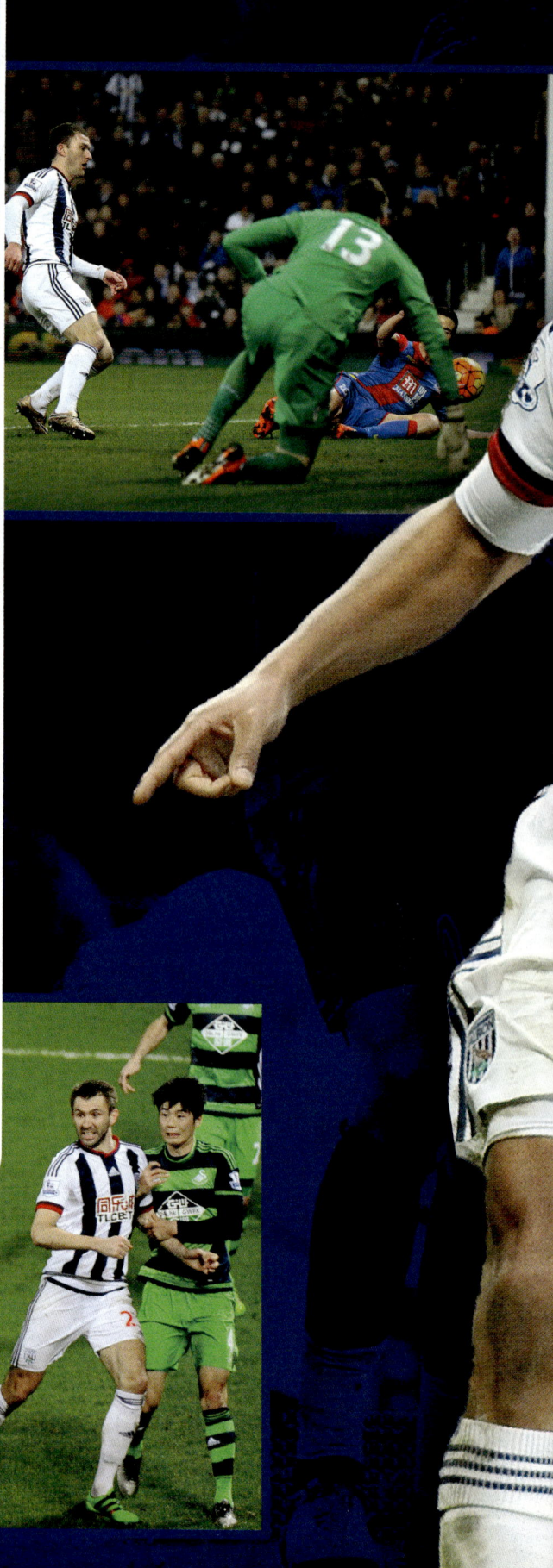

SEASON REVIEW

MARCH

Leicester were staying towards the top after all – right at the top. They were the Premier League leaders when we went there on the first day of March and played an epic end to end game that swung one way and then the other. Albion took the lead through Rondon, fell behind, then drew level with a brilliant Gardner strike from a free-kick. Two points taken off the league leaders – perfect preparation for hosting Manchester United in the next game.

Mata collected two yellow cards early in the game to get an early bath and from there, the Baggies took charge of the game, passing around United before finally getting the all-important winner, Rondon slotting past de Gea from inside the penalty area. A scruffy game ended the month, Albion beaten by a single goal at home to struggling Norwich.

SEASON REVIEW

APRIL

It's always a long trip to Sunderland – they aren't going to move it are they? – but free coaches took plenty of Baggies fans up there for the game and they were rewarded with a draw that took us to the 40 point mark and a place in the Premier League for 2016/17.

Another terrific away day display saw us push Manchester City to the limit before losing 2-1, but we hit a difficult patch through the rest of the month, losing to Watford, Arsenal and West Ham, although in the middle of that run, we did pretty much end any hopes Tottenham had of toppling Leicester and winning the league, Craig Dawson scoring at both ends in a 1-1 draw at White Hart Lane. Pizza all round from Claudio Ranieri in Leicester!

MAY

The season came to its end with a couple of 1-1 draws, away at Bournemouth and at home to Liverpool on a final day when the club paid a special tribute to the families of those who died in the Hillsborough disaster.

Things ended on a positive note with 17 year old Jonathan Leko starting the last three games in a row and impressing with his pace and trickery on the wing, while Academy graduates Sam Field and Tyler Roberts made their debuts against Liverpool.

That was the year that was – and we get to do it all over again in 2016/17!

2015/2016

DATE			OPPOSITION	SCORE	
Sat	8	Aug	MANCHESTER CITY	0-3	
Sat	15	Aug	WATFORD	0-0	
Sun	23	Aug	CHELSEA	2-3	Morrison 2
Tue	25	Aug	PORT VALE (LC2)	0-0 *(Albion won 5-3 on penalties)*	
Sat	29	Aug	STOKE CITY	1-0	Rondon
Sat	12	Sep	SOUTHAMPTON	0-0	
Sat	19	Sep	ASTON VILLA	1-0	Berahino
Wed	23	Sep	NORWICH CITY (LC3)	0-3	
Mon	28	Sep	EVERTON	2-3	Dawson, Berahino
Sat	3	Oct	CRYSTAL PALACE	0-2	
Sat	17	Oct	SUNDERLAND	1-0	Berahino
Sat	24	Oct	NORWICH CITY	1-0	Rondon
Sat	31	Oct	LEICESTER CITY	2-3	Rondon, Lambert
Sat	7	Nov	MANCHESTER UNITED	0-2	
Sat	21	Nov	ARSENAL	2-1	Morrison, Arteta (og)
Sun	29	Nov	WEST HAM UNITED	1-1	Reid (og)
Sat	5	Dec	TOTTENHAM HOTSPUR	1-1	McClean
Sun	13	Dec	LIVERPOOL	2-2	Dawson, Olsson
Sat	19	Dec	AFC BOURNEMOUTH	1-2	McAuley
Sat	26	Dec	SWANSEA CITY	0-1	
Mon	28	Dec	NEWCASTLE UNITED	1-0	Fletcher
Sat	2	Jan	STOKE CITY	2-1	Sessegnon, Evans
Sat	9	Jan	BRISTOL CITY (FA Cup 3)	2-2	Berahino, Morrison

MATCH STATS

DATE			OPPOSITION	SCORE	
Wed	13	Jan	CHELSEA	2-2	Gardner, McClean
Sat	16	Jan	SOUTHAMPTON	0-3	
Tue	19	Jan	BRISTOL CITY (FA CUP 3R)	1-0	Rondon
Sat	23	Jan	ASTON VILLA	0-0	
Sat	30	Jan	PETERBOROUGH UNITED (FA Cup 4)	2-2	Berahino 2
Tue	2	Feb	SWANSEA CITY	1-1	Rondon
Sat	6	Feb	NEWCASTLE UNITED	0-1	
Wed	10	Feb	PETERBOROUGH UNITED (FA CUP 4R)	1-1 *(Albion won 4-3 on penalties)*	Fletcher
Sat	13	Feb	EVERTON	1-0	Rondon
Sat	20	Feb	READING (FA Cup 5)	1-3	Fletcher
Sat	27	Feb	CRYSTAL PALACE	3-2	Gardner, Dawson, Berahino
Tue	1	Mar	LEICESTER CITY	2-2	Rondon, Gardner
Sun	6	Mar	MANCHESTER UNITED	1-0	Rondon
Sat	19	Mar	NORWICH CITY	0-1	
Sat	2	Apr	SUNDERLAND	0-0	
Sat	9	Apr	MANCHESTER CITY	1-2	Sessegnon
Sat	16	Apr	WATFORD	0-1	
Thu	21	Apr	ARSENAL	0-2	
Mon	25	Apr	TOTTENHAM HOTSPUR	1-1	Dawson
Sat	30	Apr	WEST HAM UNITED	0-3	
Sat	7	May	AFC BOURNEMOUTH	1-1	Rondon
Sun	15	May	LIVERPOOL	1-1	Rondon

ALL CHANGE!

CHANGE WAS IN THE AIR IN AUGUST OF 2016 WHEN ALBION ANNOUNCED THAT THE CLUB WAS PREPARING FOR A CHANGE IN OWNERSHIP.

Chairman Jeremy Peace, who has been leading the Throstles since 2002, announced that he was stepping down from that role, to be replaced by former Blackburn chairman John Williams, prior to his ownership of the club being transferred to Yunyi Guokai (Shanghai) Sports Development Limited, a company controlled by Guochuan Lai.

Mr Lai immediately stressed that his ambitions are to invest in the Club for the long-term, to maintain the hard work that has been put in over the last 14 years and to build for an even more successful future.

Mr Williams added that the immediate task was to focus on the 2016/17 season to ensure that Albion had the necessary players in the squad to help us be competitive and keep beating the likes of Manchester United!

Mr Peace wished good luck to both successors, adding that Mr Lai "has a vision for the future and the energy to see it through".

Exciting times ahead for the Albion!

DOWNLOAD ALBION!

IF YOU WANT TO KNOW ALL THERE IS TO KNOW ABOUT YOUR FOOTBALL CLUB, DON'T WORRY – WE'RE GETTING IT COVERED!

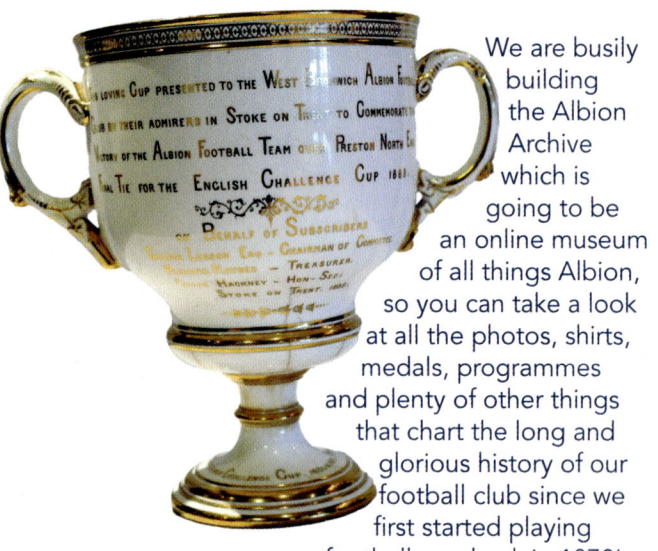

We are busily building the Albion Archive which is going to be an online museum of all things Albion, so you can take a look at all the photos, shirts, medals, programmes and plenty of other things that chart the long and glorious history of our football club since we first started playing football way back in 1878!

You will also be able to look at all the statistics from all the games and all the players, right the way back into the earliest days of the club, all the way up to the present time, from the days of Billy Bassett through to the goals of Salomon Rondon!

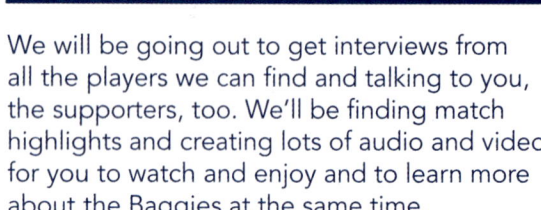

We will be going out to get interviews from all the players we can find and talking to you, the supporters, too. We'll be finding match highlights and creating lots of audio and video for you to watch and enjoy and to learn more about the Baggies at the same time.

We will be building this for years to come, but we'll be keeping you informed regularly on wba.co.uk as we put it together – make sure you keep in touch with it!

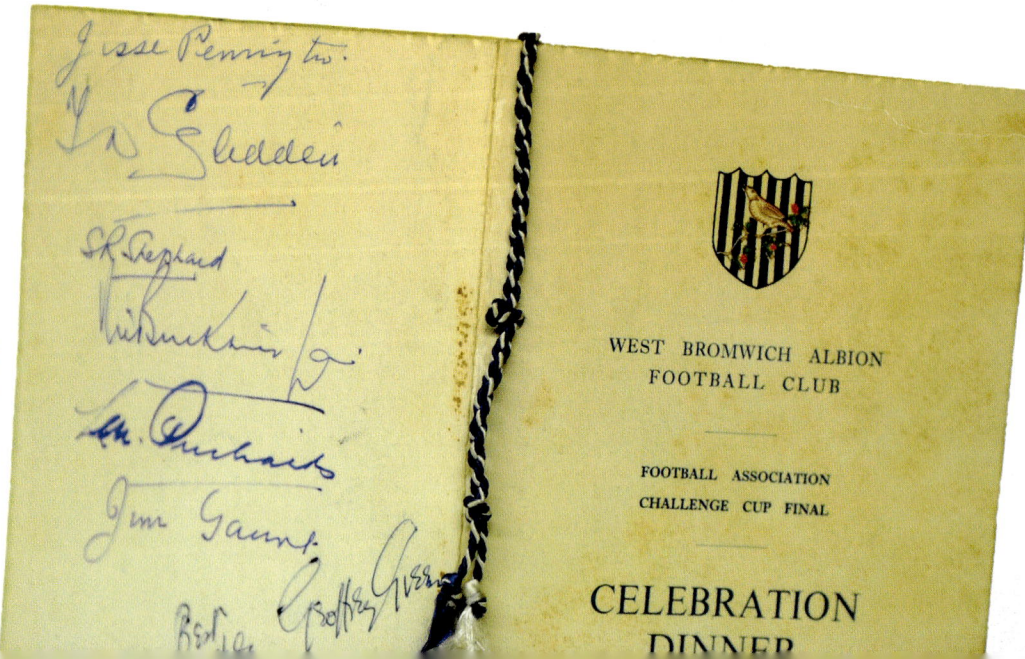

WORD SEARCH

Find the words in the grid. Words can go horizontally, vertically and diagonally in all eight directions.

ASTLE
BALIS
BARLOW
BROWN
CUNNINGHAM
EVANS
FOSTER
REGIS
ROBSON
STATHAM
WILE

Y	J	N	O	S	B	O	R	M	J
N	J	T	M	R	T	F	R	A	L
B	H	G	O	R	S	R	R	H	Q
R	L	W	E	I	M	R	N	G	N
E	N	W	L	V	S	C	H	N	H
T	R	A	O	I	A	E	L	I	J
S	B	Y	G	L	L	N	M	N	W
O	R	E	R	T	R	L	S	N	I
F	R	D	S	Q	D	A	X	U	L
S	T	A	T	H	A	M	B	C	E

Answers on p.61

DINNER PARTY...
WITH CRAIG DAWSON

THE TABLE IS LAID, THE SILVERWARE IS OUT, GLASSES ARE FILLED AND YOUR DINNER PARTY IS READY TO GO.

The doorbell rings and the first of your invited guests is at the door...but this is no ordinary Friday night gathering.

This is a fantasy dinner party whereby you are able to throw your doors open to absolutely anyone – closest family, dearest friends, movie stars, musicians, people of faith, comedians, sportspeople or even politicians.

So we sat down with Craig Dawson to see who he would invite round for the night...

1 Number one would have to be my older brother, Andy. He's someone who I've looked up to all my life and he's always there for me, he's good fun when you take him out as well.

2 Ed Sheeran – someone would have to bring the entertainment and he would be great with his guitar. I like his music.

3 Freddie Flintoff – My brother and I are cricket fans and played cricket as well so I think some of the stories he would have would be great to listen to.

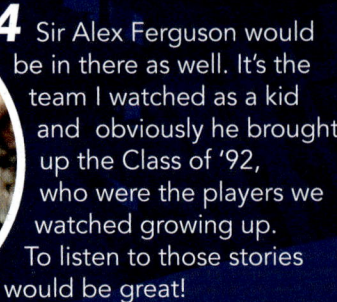

4 Sir Alex Ferguson would be in there as well. It's the team I watched as a kid and obviously he brought up the Class of '92, who were the players we watched growing up. To listen to those stories would be great!

5 Jimmy Carr would be in there because he would be listening to the stories and the comments would be coming out....his laugh as well.

6 And finally, the food...the chef would be Gordon Ramsay cooking in an open kitchen just to see what he was saying as well as cooking.

I think that would be quite entertaining. A good group.

NACER TO FLY ALBION TO THE MOON!

ALBION MADE ANOTHER ADDITION TO THEIR SQUAD WITH THE ARRIVAL OF NACER CHADLI FROM SPURS DURING THE TRANSFER WINDOW.

The 27-year-old Belgium international arrived with a reputation for pace and creativity – and in a variety of positions.

He said, "I think my best position is out on the left or maybe behind the striker. But I can play anywhere in midfield if asked.

"This is a great challenge and I want to show my quality to the fans and to the club. I just want to help the team win as many games as possible."

Chadli was eager to stay in the Premier League having enjoyed a three-season stint at Tottenham during which he scored 25 goals in 119 appearances, including three in 29 games during Spurs' acclaimed Premier League title challenge last season.

"I have learned a lot in the last three years especially how much the fans love the Premier League – that is why I was so keen to continue," he said.

"Small teams can beat big teams on any day and it's a great competition.

"I know from playing against Albion how very well organised they are and how tough they can be to beat."

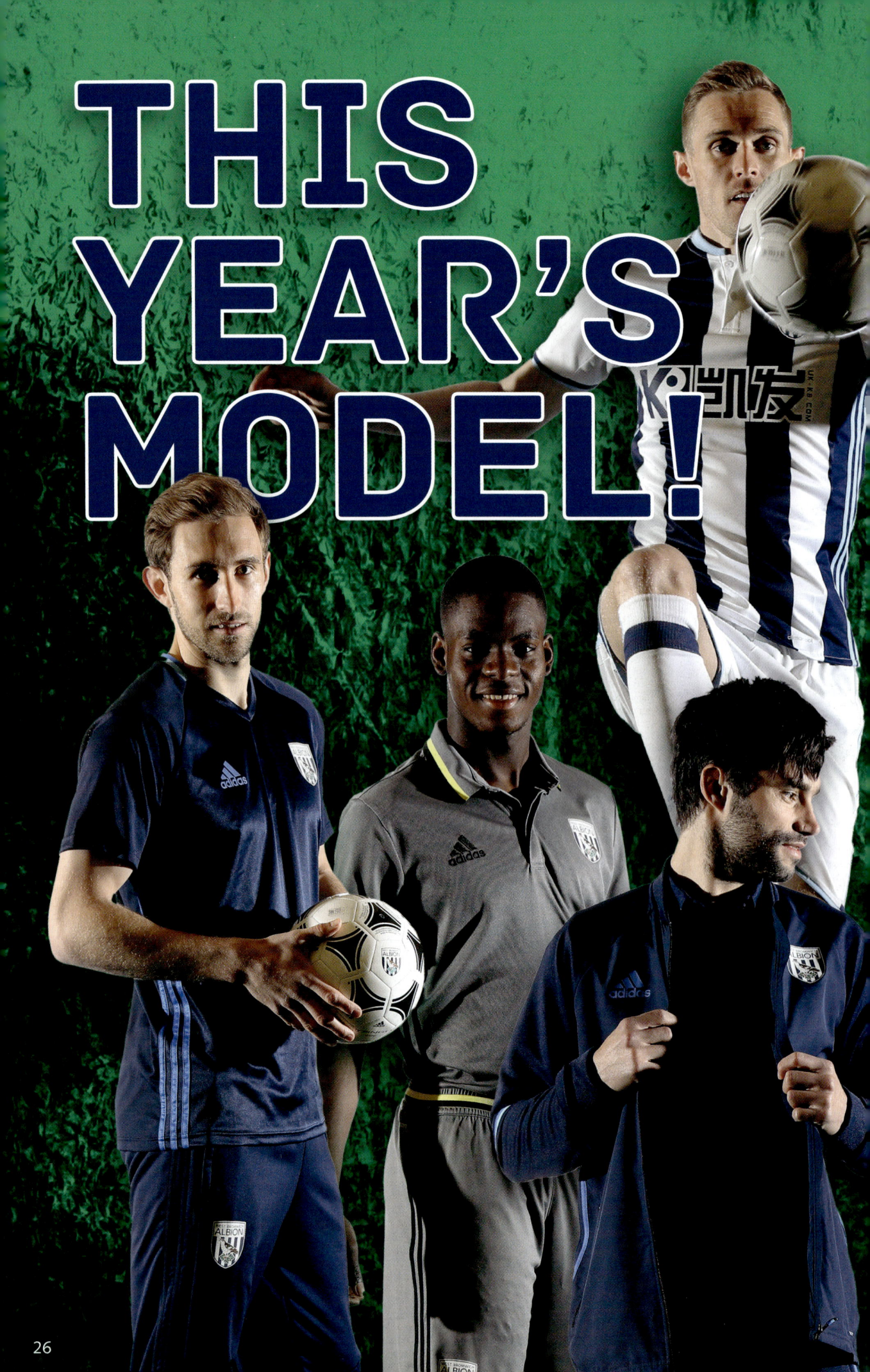

THESE DAYS, PLAYERS DON'T JUST HAVE TO DO THEIR BIT ON THE FOOTBALL FIELD –

we like them to do a few other things too.

So when we were launching the new kit and our new range of clothing for the club shop, we called on some of the boys to lend us a hand by having their photographs taken.

Modelling for us this year were Darren Fletcher, Ben Foster, Salomon Rondon, Gareth McAuley, Claudio Yacob, Craig Dawson and youngsters Jonathan Leko and Tyler Roberts.

They all did their bit for the cause but… don't give up the day job lads!

SUMMERTIME, AND

CLEARLY GERSHWIN NEVER SPENT JULY WITH TONY PULIS BECAUSE IF HE HAD, HE WOULDN'T HAVE BEEN SO SANGUINE ABOUT THE SUMMER MONTHS.

Albion's finest were put through their paces in preparation for the new campaign in Austria, the Netherlands, Spain and dear old England too and we were there to capture it, from sweating to soaking, from selfies to stretches.

THE LIVING IS EASY

Albion News went Full Throstle in 2015/16, but we don't have to spell it out to you...

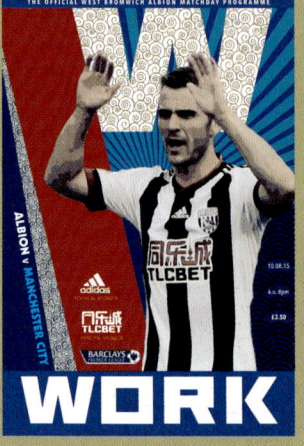

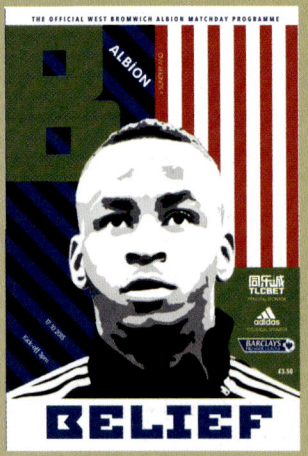
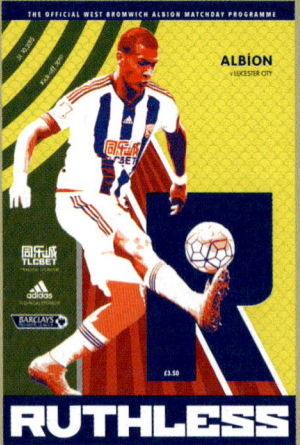

TWO PROGRAMMES FOR THE PRICE OF ONE? ONLY WITH ALBION NEWS. ONLY FOR YOU.

This season - and thanks once again for picking us up - we've given you a read like none other in the Premier League. At the front end of Albion News you've been able to enjoy exclusive interviews,  considered match reports and all the latest news from The Hawthorns. And on the flipside, in our splendid Full Throstle section featuring bespoke covers from Paine Proffitt, we've gone back through the ages and put

 call: 0845 143 0001

 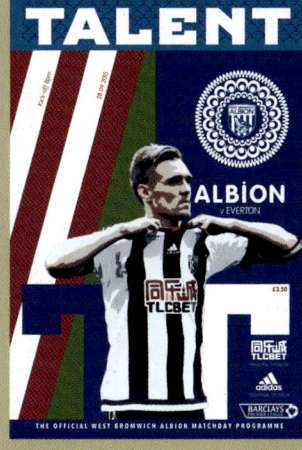

And if you've missed a copy there's still time to complete your collection....

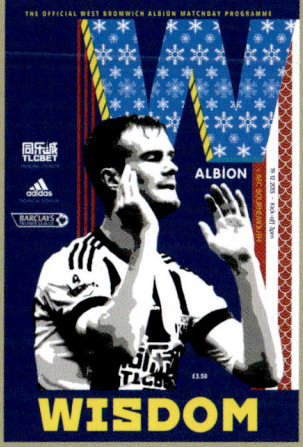 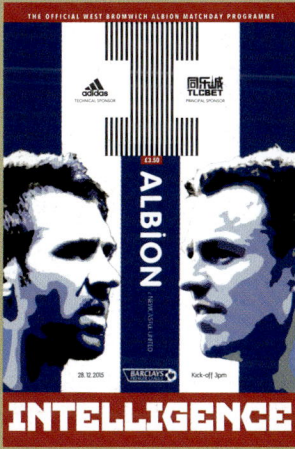  

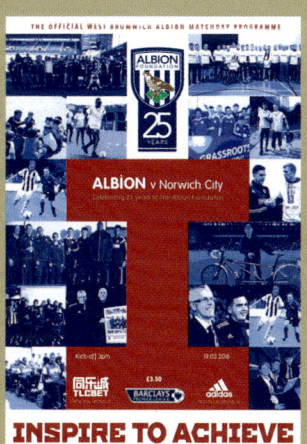   

a modern twist on Albion history with a unique nostalgia section.

As for the rather bold and eye-catching front cover deisgn, you could say it's got our name on it.

If your collection isn't complete then details of how you can get your paws on back issues can be found below, but get 'em while they last, eh?

And next season? We are Albion. We're cut from a different cloth. There's no same old, same old here. So you might just be in for a surprise in August and the good news is you can already subscribe now...

email: enquiries@sportmedia-tm.com • website: www.sportmediashop.com

Back issues available while stocks last. P&P applies. Lines open Monday to Friday 9am-5pm (excluding Bank Holidays)

PLAYER OF THE SEASON

2015/16 WAS HIS FIRST FULL SEASON AT THE HAWTHORNS BUT SKIPPER DARREN FLETCHER MADE THE ABSOLUTE MOST OF IT!

Starting every single Premier League game of the campaign, Fletcher was a model of consistency, winning the ball in the midfield, driving his team forward, setting up goals, scoring them too.

Darren was an inspirational leader of the team, keeping things ticking over and helping set new standards throughout the football club as we left behind two seasons of relegation struggles to ensure that we established our place in the Premier League for another season long before the season was over.

He was an obvious choice for the Player of the Year award, presented by the legendary Tony Brown before the final game of the season, at home to Liverpool.

Darren hasn't only made an impact on the pitch though because he has been a fantastic ambassador for the Baggies too, whether it is patiently answering hundreds of questions from the media, writing his regular column in the Albion matchday programme or going out and visiting schools and hospitals throughout the local community to spread the Albion gospel that little bit further.

Darren was a worthy winner of the Player of the Year award – and just you try and take it away from him next season!

DARREN FLETCHER

THE BIG ALBION QUIZ: THE PREMIER LEAGUE YEARS

ALBION HAVE HAD TEN FULL SEASONS IN THE PREMIER LEAGUE NOW – BUT WHAT DO YOU KNOW ABOUT EACH OF THEM? FIND OUT WITH OUR SPECIAL QUIZ!

1 **2002/03:** Who were our opponents in our first ever Premier League game?

2 **2004/05:** We achieved the "Great Escape" from relegation on the final day of the season – but which three teams went down?

3 **2005/06:** We beat Arsenal 2-1 at The Hawthorns in this season – who scored our goals?

4 **2008/09:** Which former Middlesbrough midfielder was our captain throughout this season?

5 **2010/11:** We drew 3-3 at Newcastle on the final day of the season – who scored a hat-trick for us that day?

6 **2011/12** Peter Odemwingie top scored for Albion in this season, getting one hat-trick for us – against which team?

7 **2012/13:** We got our record Premier League points total in this year – how many?

8 **2013/14:** We won our first game at Old Trafford since 1978 in this season – who was our head coach on that day?

9 **2014/15:** We lost 3-2 at home to Leicester City in April 2015, but which former goalscorer did we celebrate on that day?

10 **2015/16:** Which player made his 300th appearance for the Albion during this season?

34   Answers on p.61

ALLAN'S KEY TO ALBION HOPES

JET HEELED RIGHT-BACK ALLAN NYOM JOINED ALBION ON TRANSFER DEADLINE DAY AND THE 28 YEAR OLD WAS QUICK TO EXPRESS HIS HOPES OF BECOMING A REGULAR IN THE FIRST TEAM.

Nyom, who will wear the club's No.2 jersey, signed a four-year contract at The Hawthorns. He has experience of football in France, Italy and Spain, where he made his name in more than 200 appearances for Granada with whom he won two promotions and played regularly in La Liga.

He signed for Watford at the start of last season and played in both games against the Baggies in what proved to be a successful debut campaign.

"Last year was my first in England," he said. "I was so happy to play in the Premier League as I think it is one of the best leagues in the world. I enjoyed it a lot.

"The Premier League is completely different to other Leagues because here there is more intensity, more fight... the atmosphere in England is better than in Spain.

"The team here is good and with good players, a team that plays together. I'm going to try to bring energy and to give my best every game; I want to help the team."

HERE, THERE &

WE ARE A PRETTY WELL TRAVELLED CLUB YOU KNOW – THAT'S WHY ALBION ARE KNOWN ALL OVER THE WORLD!

Ever since our first game overseas, in Copenhagen in May 1909, against Newcastle United of all teams, we have been to all kinds of countries to play all kinds of games – we've put just a few of them on the map!

SCOTLAND:
Glasgow,
19 May 1888,
Renton 4
Albion 1

USA:
New York,
18 July 1966,
Albion 2
Kilmarnock 0

BELGIUM:
Brussels,
13 October 1954,
Albion 3
Honved 5

CANADA:
Winnipeg,
10 June 1959,
Manitoba All Stars 1
Albion 10

PORTUGAL:
Lisbon,
25 July 2005,
Sporting Lisbon 3
Albion 1

USA:
San Jose,
18 May 1990,
Albion 1
Real Madrid 6

SPAIN:
Valencia,
22 November 1978,
Valencia 1
Albion 1

PERU:
Lima,
13 May 1966,
Alianza Lima 2
Albion 3

BRAZIL:
Rio de Janeiro,
5 June 1966,
Flamengo 1
Albion 2

EVERYWHERE!

SWITZERLAND:
Zurich,
16 September 1981,
Grasshopper Zurich 1
Albion 0

DENMARK:
Odense,
15 July 2003,
Odense B1909 1
Albion 2

AUSTRIA:
Schladming,
8 July 2015,
Red Bull Salzburg 3
Albion 1

RUSSIA:
St Petersburg,
1 June 1957,
Zenit Leningrad 1
Albion 1

SERBIA:
Belgrade,
7 March 1979,
Red Star Belgrade 1
Albion 0

CHINA:
Shanghai,
22 May 1978,
Shanghai 0
Albion 2

NETHERLANDS:
Utrecht,
2 November 1966,
DOS Utrecht 1
Albion 1

GEORGIA:
Tblisi,
7 June 1957,
Dinamo Tblisi 1
Albion 3

HONG KONG:
Hong Kong,
28 May 1978,
Hong Kong Select 0
Albion 3

ROMANIA:
Bucharest,
13 November 1968,
Dinamo Bucharest 1
Albion 1

UGANDA:
Kampala,
29 May 1968,
Uganda 0
Albion 1

KENYA:
Nairobi,
8 June 1968,
Kenya 3
Albion 4

37

OUR BALL, BUT WHICH ONE?

WE'VE GOT TWO AGAINST ONE HERE AGAINST LIVERPOOL LAST SEASON, BUT NEITHER TYLER ROBERTS NOR CLAUDIO YACOB SEEM TO KNOW WHICH BALL TO GO FOR.

CAN YOU HELP THEM OUT PLEASE?!?

Answers on p.61

MY FIRST: CHRIS BRUNT

WITH 300 GAMES FOR THE ALBION BEHIND HIM, WE ASKED CHRIS BRUNT TO GO BACK TO MEMORIES OF SOME FIRSTS…

Memory of football?

Playing in the back garden with my cousin as a young boy growing up in Northern Ireland. We would be out there for hours and wouldn't really ever come in until it was dark.

Thing you do when you get to the stadium on a matchday?

I'm not getting any younger so I like to get in nice and early and see the masseurs so I am in the best possible condition for the game.

Albion game?

It was against Barnsley in 2007 shortly after I had signed. I came on as a second-half substitute and we won the game 2-0, so it was nice to start my Albion career on a winning note.

Holiday with friends?

I went to Majorca when I was about 18 with a group of mates. We had booked to go for two weeks but I could only stay for seven days because I had to go home for a hernia operation.

Expensive thing you bought?

My first car. It was a Volkswagen Polo.

Film you saw at the cinema?

I remember my parents taking me to see one of the Hook films when I was younger. I quite enjoyed it.

Time you were in trouble?

I used to get into trouble at school for climbing up on the roof to collect the footballs that my mates and I had whacked up there during lunchtimes.

Thing you do when you leave training?

It depends what time it is and what day it is to be totally honest. I don't really have a set routine. It's not very exciting, I'll either head home and sort a few bits out or pick my boys up from school.

Mobile phone?

I had a Nokia as my first phone. I forget what model it was but I do know that it had Snake on it. I used to love playing Snake, it was a great game.

Person to take the mick out of you when something goes wrong?

That's such an easy one. It is always either Mozza or Gareth. They don't let me get away with anything.

MY FAVOURITE GAME

ALBION'S GIANT SWEDISH CENTRAL DEFENDER JONAS OLSSON has played over 250 games for us, but when it came to selecting the favourite game of his career, he went for one pretty close to home – at Molineux in fact.

"The games with Sweden at the Euros were maybe the most memorable but I have mixed feelings because we didn't get through the group, whereas the 5-1 win at Wolves, that was all good! Not only was it a great win, but I had a good game too, I scored a goal, I set another one up, so it was a special day all round.

"We completely dominated the game but they scored right at half-time and we went in at 1-1. Although we were disappointed, we just had the feeling that day that nothing was going to beat us. Sometimes you just have that energy and confidence in a game and that day, we seemed to know we would win the game.

"My goal came from a set piece, it was half cleared but I was still in the box. The ball came towards me and I thought I might hit it right away, but I decided to control it. I had a good touch and then I hit it on the up bounce. I didn't connect with as much power as I wanted, but it went through a lot of players and Hennessey saw it late I think.

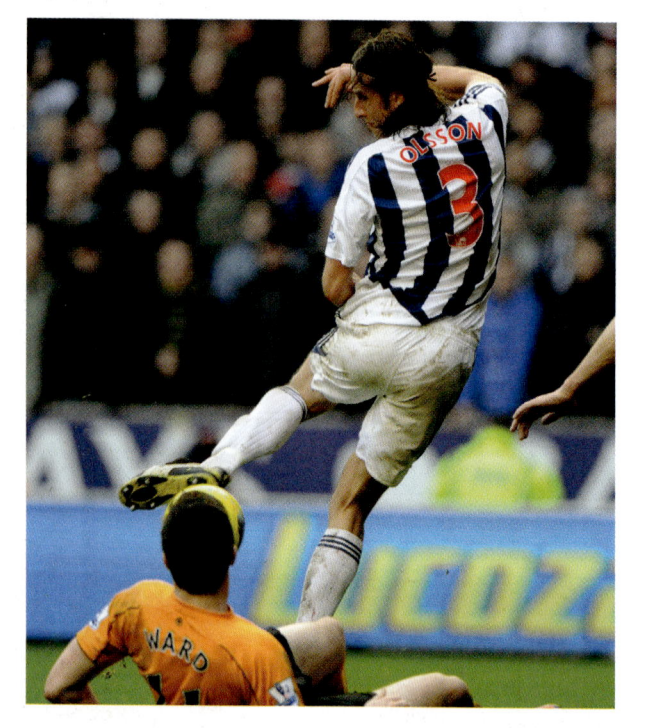

Maybe he should have done better, but that's ok, I don't mind!

"The one for Peter, that was another set piece. The ball bounced up as I was facing away from goal and I could sense Peter was behind me. I just tried to steer it towards him, it was a back heel straight to him and he was deadly from that distance!

"I had a good run in derby games, at Villa away, Birmingham at home, for some reason most of my goals have been in derby games. It's a good quality, rising to the occasion hopefully! There aren't so many derby games now, so that's why I don't score so often!

"But that Wolves game, I remember afterwards in the dressing room, we felt that was the turning point, that we didn't need to look down the table any longer, we could start to look up it, we had a platform to build on.

"Derby games, rationally they are still just three points but you shouldn't underestimate the boost and the energy you get from winning them. We beat Sunderland 4-0 a week later and we really started to grow into the season from there and finished very well".

RITE GAM

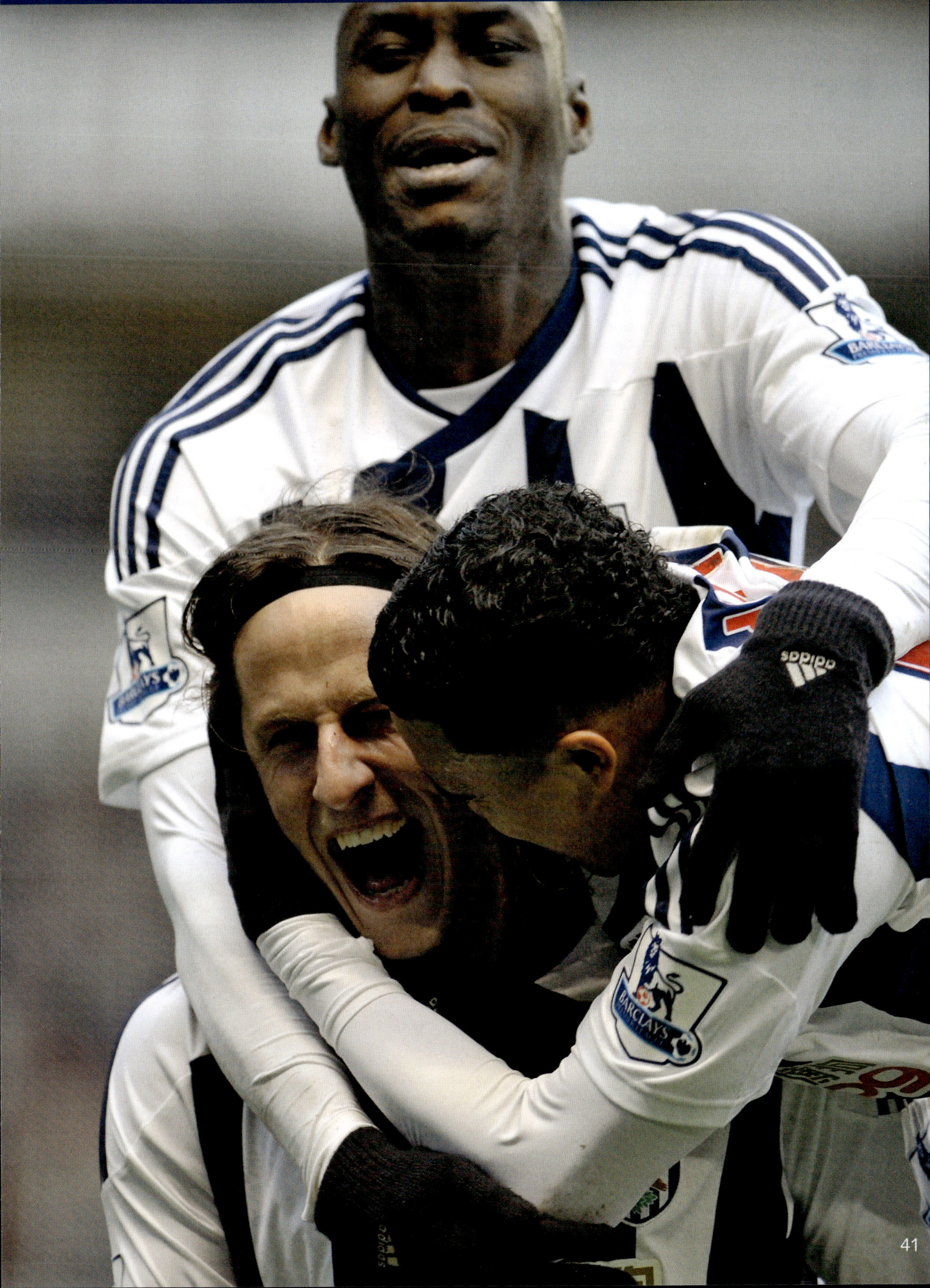

LOOKING TO MAKE HIS MARK

MATT PHILLIPS BECAME ALBION'S FIRST SIGNING OF THE SUMMER OF 2016 when he joined the Throstles in early July, a year after Albion first tried to get his signature from QPR.

Scottish international Phillips has a versatile skill-set which finds him comfortable on both flanks and as a central striker.

It was exactly that kind of football Phillips delivered on his last visit to The Hawthorns 14 months ago when he starred in a 4-1 defeat of the Baggies as QPR were fighting against relegation.

"My game is about pace, power and strength, looking to take people on, getting shots off and getting crosses in," said Phillips.

"Assists and goals - that's what I will be counting on. I want to get my place in the starting XI and build from there. But I'm not the finished article by any means. I'm 25 and I still feel I can bring more to my game.

"My last game here was when QPR were fighting for our lives to stay in the Premier League. But it seemed a great stadium with a great atmosphere and I can't wait to get out in front of the fans and show them what I can do.

"There's been a lot of speculation about this move so it is nice to get it signed off. Now I can't wait to get started."

As you can see, he went through a gruelling medical at Albion's training ground before signing for the club, so he's obviously ready to go!

HE'S ONE OF OUR OWN!

YOUNG JONATHAN LEKO CAUSED A REAL STIR IN THE PREMIER LEAGUE IN 2015/16, becoming the first player born in 1999 to play in a top flight league game when he made his debut as a sub at Manchester City.

Jonathan is a graduate of Albion's impressive academy set-up which enjoyed a fantastic end to the season with Sam Field and Tyler Roberts also making debuts for the club in the final game against Liverpool; a match which saw us fielding four academy boys, Saido Berahino making up the quartet.

But it's Jonathan who really caught the eye this year, carrying off the Young Player of the Year trophy at season's end, receiving the trophy from Academy boss Mark Harrison.

Ending the season with three terrific displays against West Ham, Bournemouth and Liverpool, setting up Salomon Rondon's goal in that game, Jonathan will be pushing hard to become a first team regular on the wing next term.

43

CLAUDIO YACOB

HE'S MAGIC, YOU KNOW!

HAL'S ON TARGET AT THE HAWTHORNS

ALBION FINISHED THEIR TRANSFER DEALINGS FOR THE SUMMER OF 2016 WHEN THEY SIGNED HAL ROBSON-KANU, ONE OF THE HEROES OF WALES' EPIC EURO 2016 CAMPAIGN, JUST BEFORE THE TRANSFER WINDOW CLOSED AT THE END OF AUGUST.

Robson-Kanu had left Reading at the end of his contract, looking to secure Premier League football and those hopes certainly weren't harmed by two goals in France as Wales made their way to the last four in Europe, Hal's cracker against Belgium voted by many as the goal of the tournament.

Hal, 27, began his career as a youngster at Arsenal before moving onto Reading where he scored 30 goals across his time with the club.

"I had some success with Wales in the summer. It was a shame that we couldn't go one step further and reach the final, but it was a great achievement all the same.

"My aim now is to get a first team place here and to score goals for the club. The biggest thing is for the club to be successful and I am really looking forward to playing my part in that over the next few seasons".

ALBION

THE EUROPEAN CHAMPIONSHIPS OF 2016

turned out to be a pretty epic occasion for the Albion players who went there with their countries, as all four made it past the group stages and into the knock-out rounds.

It looked a tough task for the Republic of Ireland when they were grouped with Italy, Belgium and Sweden, but James McClean's side gave themselves a chance right from the start by getting a draw with Sweden in their first game.

They had to beat Italy in the last game to go through, but a late Robbie Brady goal sent James and his side into the last 16 where they met France. The Irish impressed again and led at half-time, but the hosts came back to steal the win in the second half.

Gareth McAuley and Jonny Evans helped steer Northern Ireland through a tough group that included Germany, Poland and Ukraine, the key result being the victory over Ukraine when big Gareth was on the scoresheet with a powerful header. He enjoyed that one!

AT THE EUROS

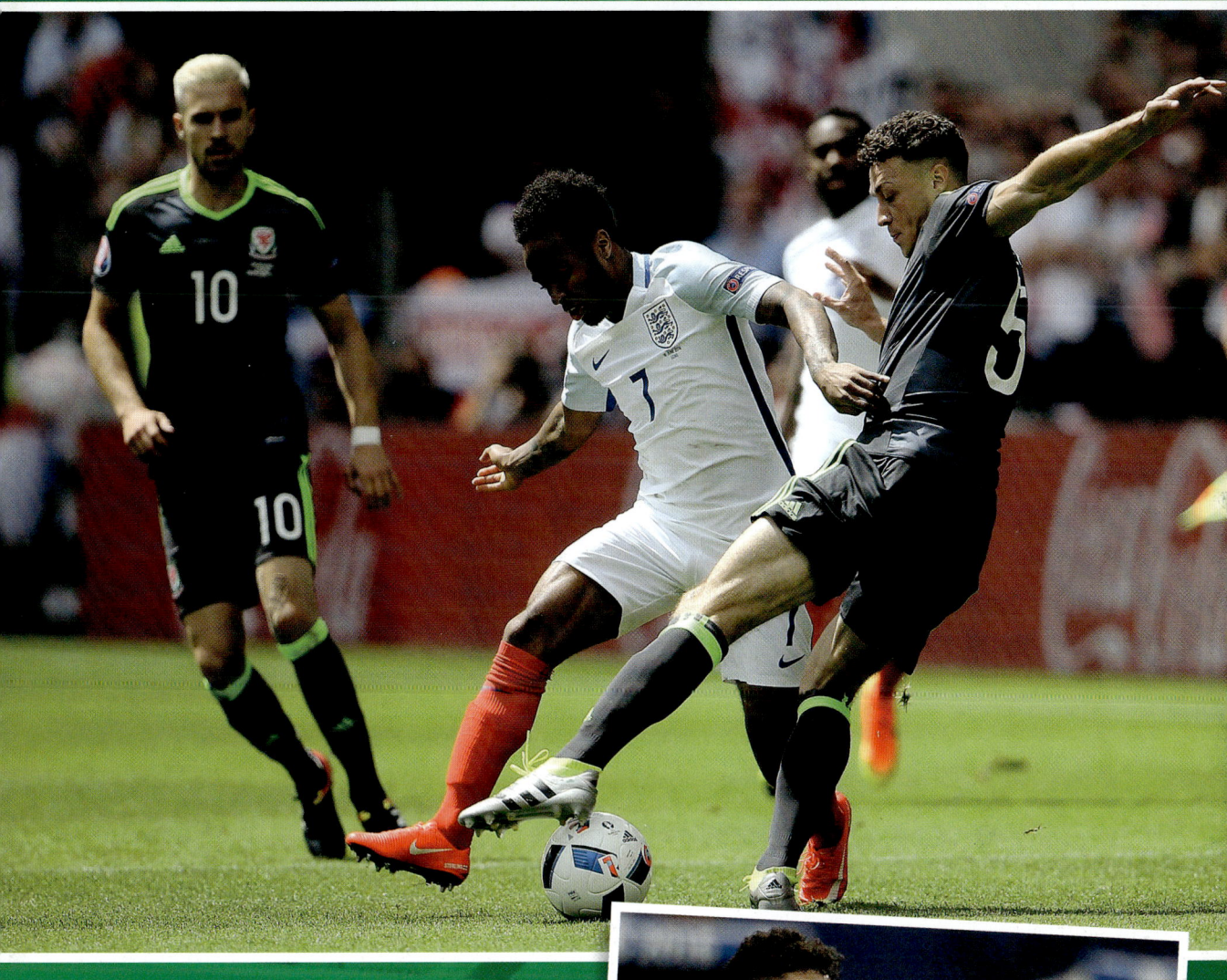

That set them up for a last 16 game with James Chester's Wales who sensationally topped their group which had included England, Slovakia and Russia.

Winning the group meant they played Northern Ireland and it was Chester who won the battle of the Baggies, Wales coming out on top 1-0 in that game. They then faced Belgium in the quarter-finals and Wales produced a stunning display to knock out one of the tournament favourites, 3-1.

Ronaldo and Portugal proved just too tough in the semi-final but nonetheless, it was a fantastic campaign for Wales, just as it was for Chester, McAuley, Evans and McClean. Good work lads!

47

BAGGIES BAG TOFFEE!

ALBION BROUGHT IN DEFENSIVE REINFORCEMENTS IN THE SHAPE OF EVERTON'S 20-YEAR-OLD LEFT-BACK DURING THE SUMMER TRANSFER WINDOW, THE HIGHLY REGARDED YOUNGSTER JOINING ON A SEASON LONG LOAN.

"I'm delighted," said Galloway, who wears the No.20 shirt. "It's a great Club and I'm really looking forward to getting started. My aims are to play and work hard for the team and help win as many matches as I can - it's all about winning.

"I think for me personally, it's really important to gain more experience. Coming here is the perfect opportunity to do that."

Galloway, born in Zimbabwe, signed a five-year deal with Premier League Everton in August 2014 having arrived from MK Dons.

The versatile defender, who can also play centre-half, made his Dons debut in November 2011 aged just 15 – the first of 17 appearance before moving to Goodison Park.

Galloway impressed for the Toffees in their Under-21 ranks and was duly handed his senior Premier League debut in May 2015 when he started a 2-1 win away at West Ham United.

But it was last season in which Galloway firmly made his first-team breakthrough – starting 14 Premier League matches as he went on to impress in 19 appearances for the Merseyside outfit, including an impressive display at The Hawthorns as Everton won 3-2.

He has represented England at Under-17, Under-18 and Under-19 level.

IT'S YOU RONDON-DON, IT'S YOU RONDON!

SUPER SALOMON RONDON ENDED HIS FIRST SEASON AT THE HAWTHORNS AS THE CLUB'S TOP GOALSCORER WITH TEN GOALS IN HIS 40 APPEARANCES IN LEAGUE AND CUP.

It was a great return for the Venezuelan international in his debut season in English football, but there's plenty more to come in the seasons ahead – that's something to look forward to isn't it?!

BAGGIES SOCCER CENTRES AND SCHOOL HOLIDAY FOOTBALL CAMPS IN DUDLEY, SANDWELL AND WORCESTER AIMED AT SCHOOL YEARS RECEPTION - YEAR 6.

Designed to help young people to have fun and develop their existing skills.

www.thealbionfoundation.co.uk

Phone: 0871 271 9840 | @WBAFoundation | f The-Albion-Foundation

THE KEY QUESTION!

NO WONDER BEN FOSTER LOOKS FED UP – SOMEBODY HAS HIDDEN HIS CAR KEYS AND HE CAN'T GET HOME AFTER TRAINING.

We reckon the dressing room joker Craig Gardner has hidden them – he looks like he's admitting it – but he's not telling Ben where they are.

Can you help find them for him?

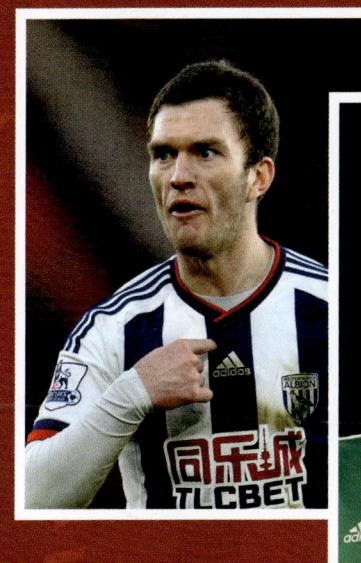

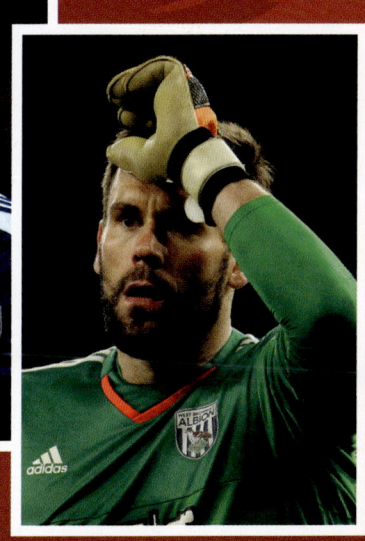

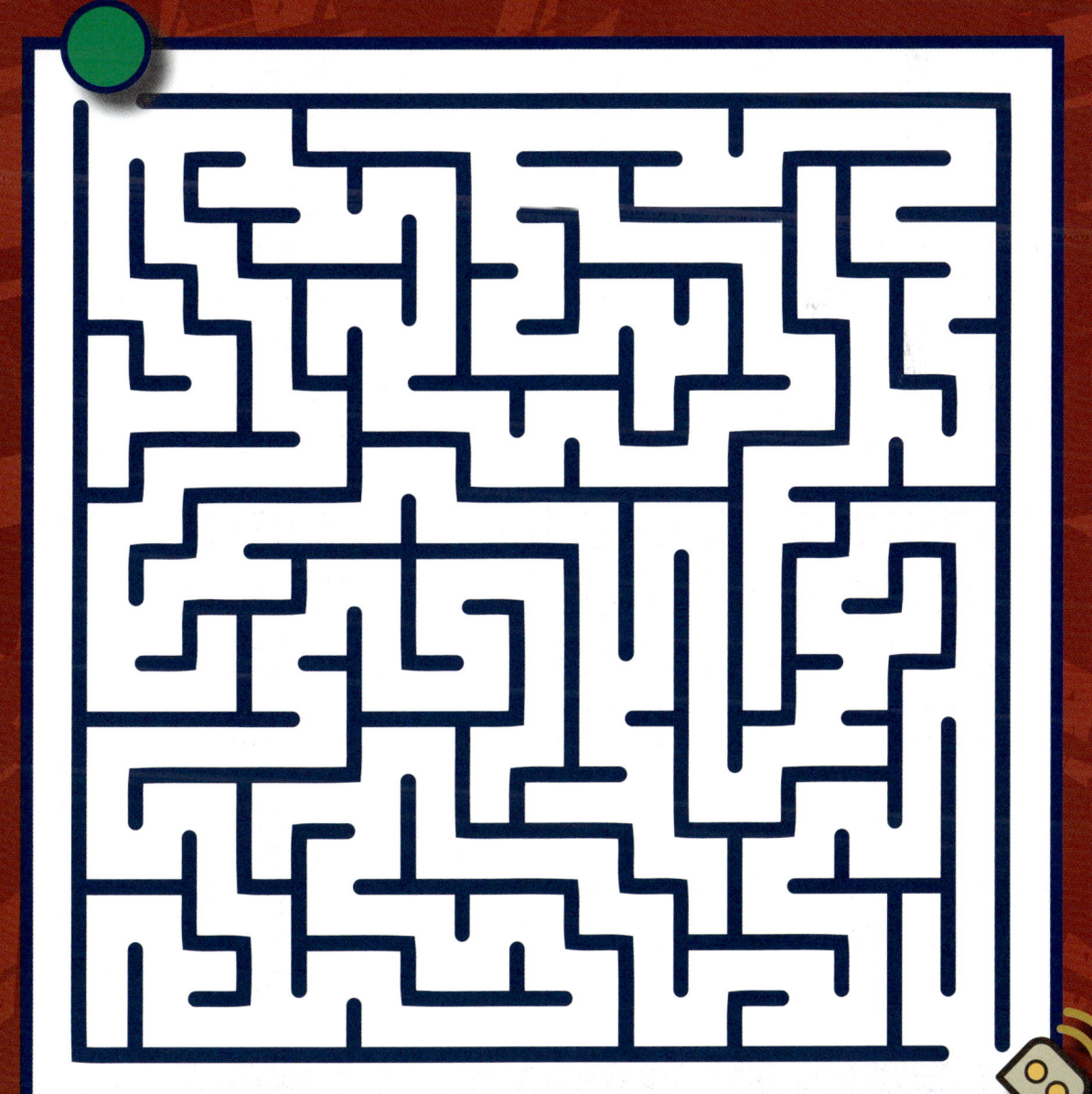

Answers on p.61

PLAYER PROFILES

BEN FOSTER

Birthdate:	3 April 1983
Position:	Goalkeeper
Height:	1.93m
Other clubs:	Stafford Rangers, Stoke City, Manchester United, Birmingham City
Albion games:	143+1
Albion goals:	0

BOAZ MYHILL

Birthdate:	9 November 1982
Position:	Goalkeeper
Height:	1.91m
Other clubs:	Aston Villa, Hull City
Albion games:	77+1
Albion goals:	0

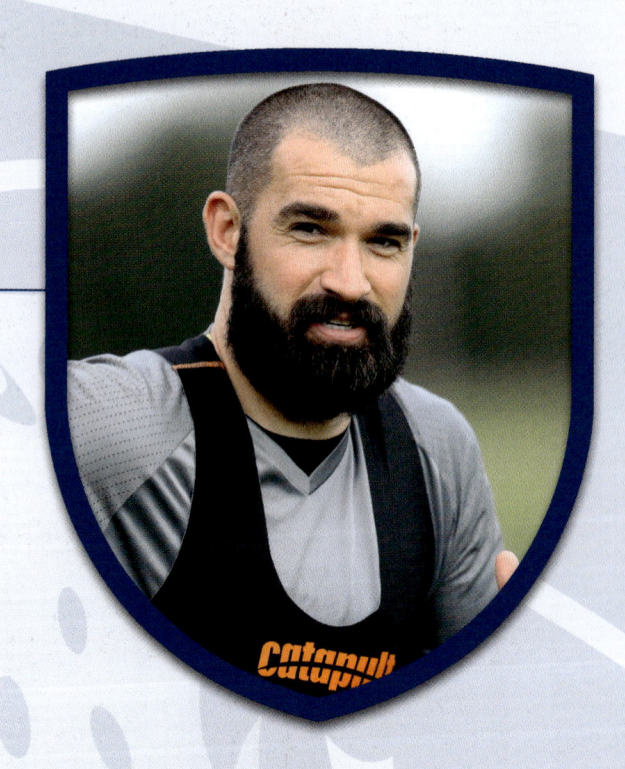

JACK ROSE

Birthdate:	31 January 1995
Position:	Goalkeeper
Height:	1.90m
Other clubs:	None
Albion games:	0
Albion goals:	0

JONAS OLSSON

Birthdate: 10 March 1983
Position: Central defender
Height: 1.93m
Other clubs: Landskrona, NEC Nijmegen
Albion games: 244+8
Albion goals: 14

JONNY EVANS

Birthdate: 3 January 1988
Position: Central defender
Height: 1.89m
Other clubs: Manchester United
Albion games: 34
Albion goals: 1

GARETH McAULEY

Birthdate: 5 December 1979
Position: Central defender
Height: 1.95m
Other clubs: Coleraine, Lincoln City, Leicester City, Ipswich Town
Albion games: 176+1
Albion goals: 10

PLAYER PROFILES

CRAIG DAWSON

Birthdate: 6 May 1990
Position: Central defender
Height: 1.88m
Other clubs: Rochdale
Albion games: 100+9
Albion goals: 7

KANE WILSON

Birthdate: 11 March 2000
Position: Left-back
Height: 1.80m
Other clubs: None
Albion games: 0
Albion goals: 0

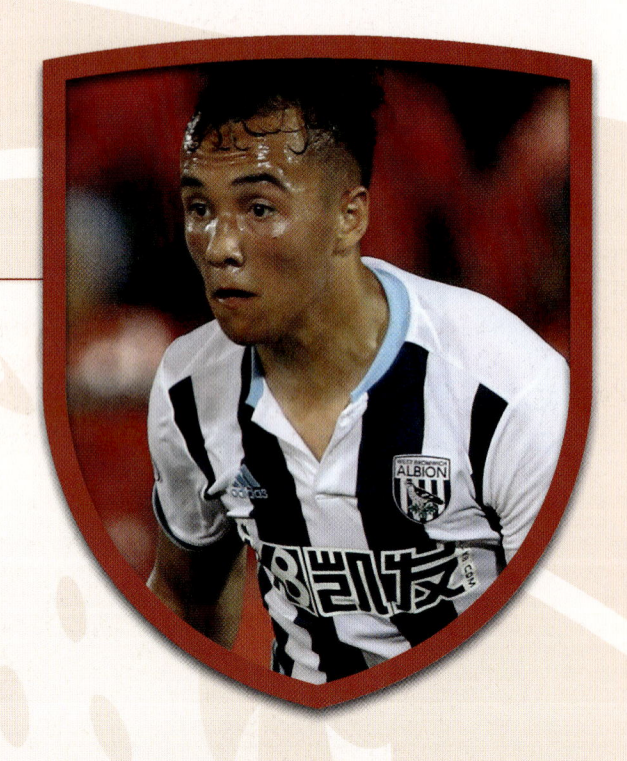

NACER CHALDI

Birthdate: 2 August 1989
Position: Winger
Height: 1.89m
Other clubs: AGOVV Apeldoorn, FC Twente, Tottenham Hotspur
Albion games: 0
Albion goals: 0

ALLAN NYOM

Birthdate:	10 May 1988
Position:	Right-Back
Height:	1.88m
Other clubs:	Arles-Avignon, Udinese, Granada, Watford
Albion games:	0
Albion goals:	0

CLAUDIO YACOB

Birthdate:	18 July 1987
Position:	Central midfielder
Height:	1.81m
Other clubs:	Racing Club de Avellaneda
Albion games:	111+12
Albion goals:	1

CHRIS BRUNT

Birthdate:	14 December 1984
Position:	Winger / left-back
Height:	1.87m
Other clubs:	Sheffield Wednesday
Albion games:	272+42
Albion goals:	42

PLAYER PROFILES

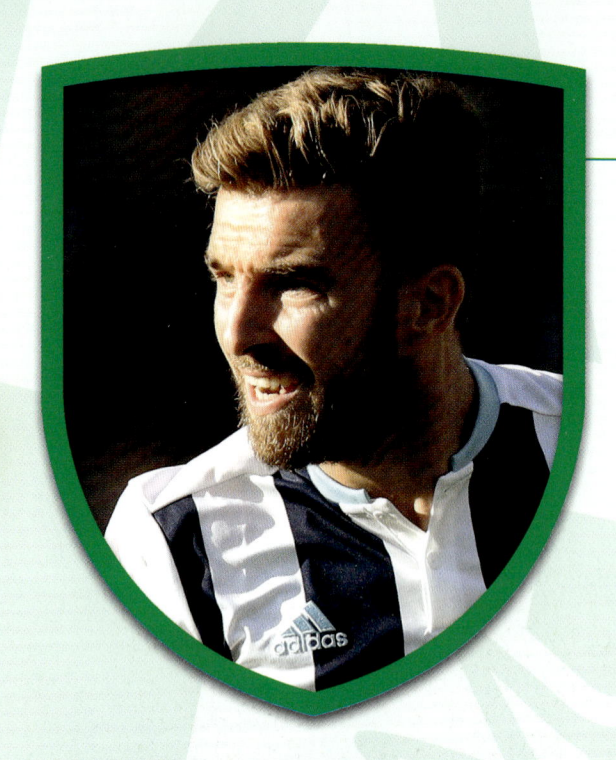

JAMES MORRISON

Birthdate: 25 May 1986
Position: Central midfielder
Height: 1.80m
Other clubs: Middlesbrough
Albion games: 227+51
Albion goals: 32

CRAIG GARDNER

Birthdate: 25 November 1986
Position: Central midfielder
Height: 1.76m
Other clubs: Aston Villa, Birmingham City, Sunderland
Albion games: 57+19
Albion goals: 6

CALLUM McMANAMAN

Birthdate: 25 April 1991
Position: Winger
Height: 1.75m
Other clubs: Wigan Athletic
Albion games: 7+17
Albion goals: 0

DARREN FLETCHER

Birthdate:	1 February 1984
Position:	Midfielder
Height:	1.83m
Other clubs:	Manchester United
Albion games:	57
Albion goals:	4

JONATHAN LEKO

Birthdate:	24 April 1999
Position:	Winger
Height:	1.82m
Other clubs:	None
Albion games:	3+3
Albion goals:	0

JAMES McCLEAN

Birthdate:	22 April 1989
Position:	Winger
Height:	1.80m
Other clubs:	Derry City, Sunderland, Wigan Athletic
Albion games:	34+8
Albion goals:	2

PLAYER PROFILES

MATT PHILLIPS

- **Birthdate:** 13 March 1991
- **Position:** Winger
- **Height:** 1.85m
- **Other clubs:** Wycombe, Blackpool, QPR
- **Albion games:** 0
- **Albion goals:** 0

SAM FIELD

- **Birthdate:** 8 May 1998
- **Position:** Midfielder
- **Height:** 1.88m
- **Other clubs:** None   Sunderland
- **Albion games:** 0+1
- **Albion goals:** 0

SALOMON RONDON

- **Birthdate:** 16 September 1989
- **Position:** Striker
- **Height:** 1.90m
- **Other clubs:** Aragua, Las Palmas, Malaga, Rubin Kazan, Zenit St Petersburg
- **Albion games:** 34+6
- **Albion goals:** 10

PROFILES

SAIDO BERAHINO

Birthdate:	4 August 1993
Position:	Striker
Height:	1.80m
Other clubs:	None
Albion games:	71+45
Albion goals:	36

HAL ROBSON-KANU

Birthdate:	21 May 1989
Position:	Striker
Height:	1.85m
Other clubs:	Reading
Albion games:	0
Albion goals:	0

TYLER ROBERTS

Birthdate:	12 January 1999
Position:	Striker
Height:	1.80m
Other clubs:	None
Albion games:	0+1
Albion goals:	0

GOAL OF THE SEASON

ALBION'S GOAL OF 2015/16 WAS SCORED BY SAIDO BERAHINO IN OUR 3-2 WIN OVER CRYSTAL PALACE AT THE HAWTHORNS – AND A BEAUTY IT WAS TOO!

We were already 2-0 up by then before we crowned a great first half with this little cracker. Craig Dawson and Salomon Rondon combined to give the ball out to Stephane Sessegnon on the Albion right.

He flighted a cross over 50 yards into the centre of the Palace area where Saido dashed in between the Palace defenders and, at full stretch, steered a first time volley away from goalkeeper Hennessey and into the corner of the net from ten yards out.

What a finish!

QUIZ AND PUZZLE ANSWERS

P.7 WORDSEARCH

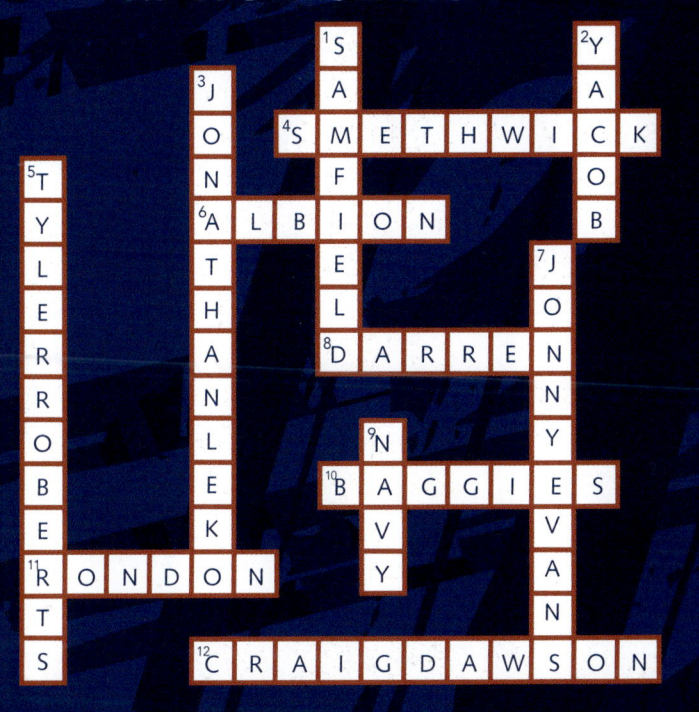

Across:
4. SMETHWICK
6. ALBION
8. DARREN
10. BAGGIES
11. RONDON
12. CRAIGDAWSON

Down:
1. SAFFELL
2. YACOB
3. JONATHANLEEK
5. TYLERROBERTS
7. JONNYEVAN
9. NAVY

P.38 WHICH BALL?

5

P.23 WORDSEARCH

P.51 THE KEY QUESTION

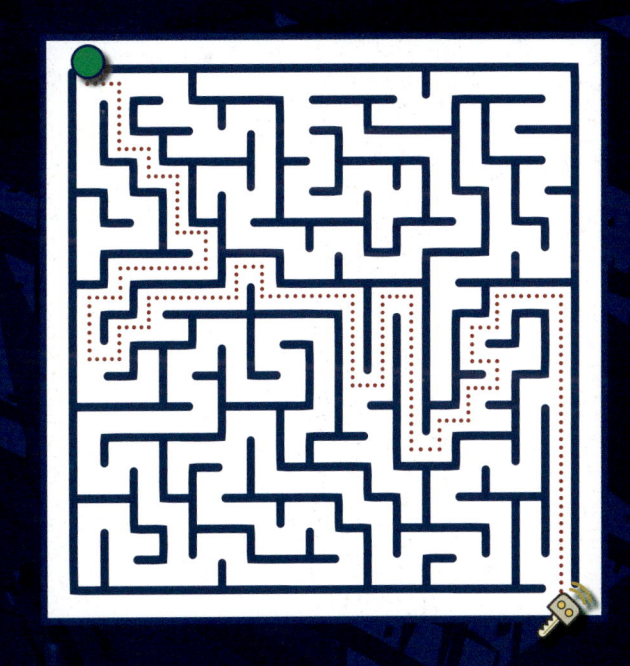

P.34 THE BIG ALBION QUIZ

1. Manchester United (away, lost 1-0)
2. Crystal Palace, Southampton and Norwich City
3. Kanu and Darren Carter
4. Jonathan Greening
5. Somen Tchoyi
6. Wolves (away, won 5-1)
7. 49
8. Steve Clarke
9. Jeff Astle on Astle Day
10. Chris Brunt

62